T0297483

Balboa Press books may be ordered through booksellers or by contacting:

Balboa Press
A Division of Hay House
1663 Liberty Drive
Bloomington, IN 47403
www.balboapress.com.au
AU TFN: 1 800 844 925 (Toll Free inside Australia)
AU Local: 0283 107 086 (+61 2 8310 7086 from outside Australia)

ISBN: 978-1-5043-2356-7 (sc)
ISBN: 978-1-5043-2355-0 (e)

Print information available on the last page.

Balboa Press rev. date: 04/13/2021

A DIVISION OF HAY HOUSE

The Adventures of
Alchemy & Aloe

Volume I
The Law of Non-Resistance

Dedication

This book is dedicated to you, me and all that have been and all that will be. But most importantly, my inner being for guiding me on my path of least resistance as I remember my truth and allow my inner magic to flow through these very words.

Acknowledgment

Thank you to all of the children that have reminded me of who I am along my journey. Now it's my turn to help you remember as you step out into this world of unlimited, ever-evolving creation.

One day, Alchemy & Aloe were riding around the neighbourhood on Alchemy's favourite red bike. He waved to a bird to say "good morning" but as he let go of the handle bars….

CRASH! Alchemy hit a rock and was flung into the air! Both Alchemy and Aloe landed safely however the bike… not so much.

"Oh no!" said Alchemy, "my wheel!"

Alchemys' wheel was busted with a biiiiig hole in it and as he looked at the wheel, he thought to himself…

"Will I have to carry my bike home?...

Just then, Aloe noticed the big cloud of fuzzy thoughts swirling around Alchemy's head. "WOAH, slow down Alchemy! You're making a mess with all of your fuzzies!"

"Sorry Aloe, I just can't seem to think of a way to help us get home", said Alchemy.

"That's because your fuzzy thoughts are in the way, Alchemy. Your thoughts are kind of like seeds that grow the more you think about them. And when you're growing fuzzy seeds all over your mind, it makes it pretty cloudy up there and harder for you to see the answer. But when you relax, and let all the fuzzies fade away, the answer will be right there ready for you. You might have heard some adults call our fuzzy thoughts *resistance* and call our rosy thoughts *non-resistance*.

So let's try to fade those fuzzies... take a deep breath in and breathe all the way out."

Alchemy gave Aloe an odd look. "Breathing slowly isn't going to fix my wheel Aloe."

"No, but breathing will relax you and when you're relaxed, you will know the answer you need to get home!"

Alchemy wasn't sure this would work however he decided to trust Aloe and try it. He closed his eyes and took a big breath in and as he breathed out something happened.

Alchemy's body started to feel light and different and as he relaxed even more, Alchemy felt an idea pop into his mind with a voice telling him to 'walk'.

"Woah, what was that?" said Alchemy. "I was breathing and then all of a sudden I feel like I should be walking."

"Is that feeling to walk a Rosy or Fuzzy feeling Alchemy?" asked Aloe.

"Hmmmm it doesn't feel fuzzy at all, so it's definitely rosy." said Alchemy.

"Well then that's Source!" said Aloe with great excitement.

"What do you mean Source, who is Source?" Said Alchemy.

"Well, Source is the invisible part of you that holds all of the answers for when you're ready to see them. Source is always ready to give them to you however you just can't hear them or see them when you're being resistant. So, now that you're relaxed, let's try this new idea to go for a walk and at the same time, I want you to ask yourself and Source, 'how can I fix my bike?'" It's very important you relax and trust there is an answer while focusing on that question, 'how can I fix my bike?'

Alchemy listened to what Aloe said and trusted that Source will provide the answer. As he began walking, he breathed slowly and relaxed whilst thinking about the question. He repeated it in his head, "how can I fix my bike… how can I fix my bike… how can I fix my bike… "

Not too far ahead, in the front yard of his neighbours home, Alchemy noticed a shiny black object was sparkling in the sun.

As he got closer, the shiny object was in fact… A BIKE WHEEL!

Alchemy ran over to see that the wheel had a little price tag on it saying $10.
He thought to himself…

I will have to carry my bike home…

What if I don't make it before dark?…

What will I eat?…

WHAT IF *I* GET EATEN BY A…."

And as Alchemy said those fuzzy words, they started to make him upset.

Aloe said, "Remember Alchemy, there is ALWAYS an answer to everything! Now before those fuzzies get any bigger, why don't you try changing your question to, 'how can I pay for this wheel?' We've made it this far already and I know you can do it Alchemy!"

So Alchemy continued looking at the wheel, relaxed and asked "how can I pay for this wheel, how can I pay for this wheel, how can I pay for this wheel?" Just then, Alchemy heard the neighbours dog barking and PING! He had another idea.

He knocked on the door of the house with the wheel out the front and waited for someone to answer.

"Yes?" Said Alchemy's neighbour, as he opened the front door.

"Hello sir! I saw your bike wheel for sale for $10 and I also heard that you have a dog in your backyard. If you let me have this bike wheel, I'll walk your dog everyday for 7 days."

The neighbour looked at Alchemy and had a long hard think….

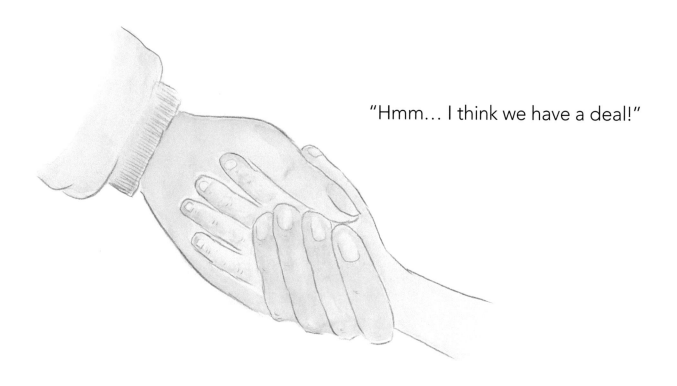

"Hmm… I think we have a deal!"

The neighbour shook Alchemy's hand and helped him put the bike wheel onto his bike.

Alchemy rode home with the biggest smile on his face and the neighbours dog running beside him. He took the dog for a walk everyday like he promised, and after 7 days he told the neighbour that he enjoyed walking the dog so much that he'd like to keep walking the dog every day after that!

"So even though your wheel breaking seemed like a disaster at first Alchemy, you were able to trust the magic you have inside by figuring out a way to get us home and were not only rewarded with a new bike wheel, but a new friend too."

Q+A & Discussion Points to utilise in conversation after the Story:

Q:What did you think of the story?
A: Open ended - let them answer freely.

Q:Do you remember the kind of thoughts Alchemy has?
A: Rosy thoughts and Fuzzy thoughts.

Q: What do those thoughts mean?
A: Rosy - Positive, happy, uplifting thoughts.
Fuzzy - Negative, sad, unhelpful thoughts.

Q: Is there anything you need help with right now?
A: If they answer no, move onto Activity 1 however if they answer yes, strategise a question together that they could ask in their head that would offer inspiration or an idea to come to mind.
See **'Activity 2: Asking for help'** for further details

Now let's put that learning into ACTION!

Activity 1: Planting seeds

After reading the story, spend some time planting seeds in your garden with your child/ children and reiterate the illustrations of the comparison of our thoughts to seeds. Having the illustrations on display and referring to them as you explain and put this in a real life scenario will bring the story to life and allow your child to understand in much simpler, practical terms. This topic can at times come across as challenging to explain, however the importance is that the seeds are planted in your child's mind and are subconsciously growing into understanding. The more you read and put the stories into practical use, the more you will see results on the outside. Remember, creation is an inside job and just because you can't see it, doesn't mean it's not there.

Activity 2: Asking for help

Brainstorm with your child/children some open ended questions that they can ask whenever they need assistance. This is subconsciously setting up communication with their infinite intelligence and infinite potential. By simply asking the question, "How can I _**problem needs solving here**___" then we open ourselves up to other frequencies and that 'outside the box' thinking. It's open ended therefore it allows endless ideas of inspiration to flow to you. This will be extra beneficial during their schooling if any tasks or problems arise. Building their confidence to know they can handle any situation, as long as they ask and having that faith that Source/the Universe/God/their inner guidance system will provide the answer.

Love, light and blessings to you all xo

Printed in the United States
by Baker & Taylor Publisher Services